THE
YALE SERIES OF YOUNGER POETS

THE WHITE GOD AND OTHER POEMS

AMS PRESS
NEW YORK

The White God and Other Poems

THOMAS CALDECOT CHUBB

NEW HAVEN · YALE UNIVERSITY PRESS

LONDON · HUMPHREY MILFORD · OXFORD UNIVERSITY PRESS

MDCCCCXX

150874

THE author makes grateful acknowledgment to the *Horae Scholasticae*, the *New Republic*, the *S-for-N*, the *Yale Literary Magazine*, and the YALE UNIVERSITY PRESS for permission to reprint here such poems as have already appeared in their pages.

TO
MY MOTHER.

TABLE OF CONTENTS.

LYRICS AND SHORTER PIECES.

SONG.

I THOUGHT of song as a trivial thing,
A toy for my hand,
A glittering pendant of tinsel,
A handful of sand,
—But lo! I have striven to sing and song is a terrible brand!

I dreamed of song as a pleasaunce
To lighten the hour,
A catch of the leaves' refrain,
And earthly dower,
—Behold! The heavens fall down and the sky is cracked by
its power!

I longed for song as a stream
That would splash for me,
A ripple adown the hillside,
A melody,
—And now it is one with the river and the river has flowed to
the sea!

The mountains arise at its sounding,
The sky is dark'd with rain,
And the lands that were sunk in the ocean
Stand up again,
—But the heart of the singer is broken for song is more bitter
than pain!

COLCHIS.

(An Argonaut Speaks.)

Yes! I can remember the hopeless seas,
  Our dripping oars that beat to foam,
The tortuous blue Symplegades,
And our distant pale home;
The fog that crawled in from the gray
Unfeeling sweep of some Dacian bay;
And Aeolus shrieking over all;
—This like a ghost, I recall!
With night after starless night of pain,
And day after drizzling day of rain;
And terrible conflict where the rocks
Lifted like Titans against the sky
To shatter us, and appalling shocks
As our helpless keel grated by;
Tugging that reddened our horny hands,
Sweat that blurred the hills into bands
Of color!—We must have quarreled too,
For I can hear loud jangling words,
—Strident as hovering harsh sea birds—
And our fingers were bleeding and blue!

The promontory at length we cleared;
The loud gale left us; north we steered,
Northward then eastward into a haze
Coppery in the sun's quenched blaze;
And so we drifted for many days—
Days that were worse than the strangling night,
For the fog oozed a venomous blight,
And the creaking strakes grew spongy-green,
And the scum of the sea had an oily sheen.

Then just at dawn the navarch died.
I remember we cast him overside,
Spinning him out with a lifeless swing;
There was one white flash of his livid face.
Then plop! died the ugly waves in a ring,
With not a ripple to mark the place!

And after, for three days white and blank,
We pitched and rolled like a rotting plank.
Till all my senses swooned away. . . .

In a dazzling flash came return of day!
And I heard Jason laugh and shout.
Then a trample of feet and a clattering rout
Of triumph—paeans and windy hymns.
Today my memory breaks or dims
To recollect that exultant hour
When I saw the sunlight redly poured,
And the land before like a sparkling sword,
And the toppled hills, and one marble tower
Of Colchis afar!

           And I know, from then
We lashèd at our sweeps with more strength than men,
And the waves streamed past us in hissing fire,
And our galley moved to the chant of a choir!

O the strange craft that seemed as friends
In our wildered relief that the voyage ends!
And the weird dusk folk that blackened the shore!
And the cry of welcome, a hideous roar!
That we loved as we did this ominous place,
And the sinister cliffs of the awful haven!

Why even Medea's evil face
Seemed richly and cleanly graven!

CLYTEMNESTRA.

"O HELEN, HELEN! 'seemeth thou'rt too fair;
'Seemeth thou art too fair, too beautiful,
My little sister! Now the gusts blow free
Thy loose robes, and I think thou art too fair,
Too fair, too sadly fair. Each balanced line
Sweeps in a modulated symmetry,
Each thin fold of thy dress, each sculptured limb—
But O what sculpture hath the dangerous fire
And fervor! 'Seemeth men crowd round and blood
Heats for thy touch, and thy fair face so cool
And warm and glorious. 'Seemeth strong men rise,
Made passionate and noble, and despairing
And treacherous—yea! these things, these shall be
In multitudinous men! And 'seemeth towers
Burn like brave beacons red against the sea.
And thou dost weep, and thou dost then forget
The little laughing things thou say'st to me.
And thou dost sudden grow noble and sudden grow
Haughty and far and full of proud desires
That none may know and live. And thou dost stand
Later, the withering South Wind in thy hair
Still bright with one bright poppy, and dost see
Paris lurch down, and lustful Menelaus
Reclaim thee with a leer; and thou dost turn
To him, and all the shrivelling years grow blank,
And thou dost pale beside him, and dost forget
The sunlight on our faces, and these flags
Rippled by the gusts as we walk hand in hand
Today, my little sister,—ere the world
Drags in upon us. And then thou dost die,
Unmindful of thy beauty, and these things,
Unmindful of thy life and love and me. . . .

". . . O Helen, Helen, Helen! thou'rt too fair,
Walking beside the lake with me today.
Beauty is God, the poets sing. I sing
That too much beauty, too much God is death.
And death is pain, and soul-obliteration.

16

Pity is me! Thou'rt beautiful, and I
Who walk beside, foreknow the ruining hand;
Foreknow that thou and earth and god are death!
And death is earth and thee, O Helen, Helen!"

OUR SHIP.

FAIREST spruce for the hull,
　Shaven and planed,—
We fashioned her beautiful—
　Evenly grained;

Pine for the spiry mast;
　Sputtering oak
Heaped for the forge's blast;
　—Our sledges spoke!

Staunchly we built her—proud,
　Shapely and swift;
Her bow the waves would crowd,
　Frothing to lift.

Bull's hide we scraped and sheared,
　Bull's thews we trimmed—
Little the gale she feared,
　Powerfully limbed.

Last on her gashing prow,
　Brazen and dire,
Hammered a beak; and now
　Trued it with fire.

Then down the blazing ways
　Into the sea,
Launched her with all our praise
　Wonderfully.

Fitted her out with men,
　King's sons and tall;
Loud was the song that then
　Rose from us all.

Into the western mist,
　Wake fire to burn,
Sailed she. . . . Some yet persist
　She will return!

THE *OLYMPIA*.

ALL through the rusting shipyards the bated whisper runs—
Wars and rumors of fighting, battles, and men, and
guns;
From the creaking rudders below them to the weathered masts
of the ships,
There's a thrill and a new-born ardor, and a talk of war on
their lips.
The sound of the chattering hammers the city echoes awoke:
In the stir of the dreadnaughts fitting out, the old *Olympia*
spoke—

"Well I remember that evening—the time I headed the line—
The moon was under a jagged cloud, and the air was chilly
and fine.
Onward we swept through the mine-fields with never a lan-
tern to burn,
And never a sound, a whisper, save the murmur around our
stern.
A reckless battery saw us and loudly it voiced its ire:
Mind ye how sharply I silenced it in a storm of shot and fire.

"Well I remember the morning. Unrippled the streaky bay;
The graceful palms by the water lifted against the day;
The yellow banner of Philip challenged the yellow sun;
Till I—ah how I remember—fired my warning gun.

"All through the placid morning, over Manila Bay
My spinning shells went screeching up, onward upon their
way.
The thin white splashes slopped upward, as the shattering
hail beat down.
A ceaseless roar the hills awoke over the drowsy town.
Their ships and the forts gave answer, but little I recked their
guns—
Who fires the truest never is hurt; nor firing oftenest runs.
My guns belched noisy anger and their clamor was not in vain:
For they sent the fleet of the Spanish King under the Spanish
Main."

The hammers ended their tapping; the whistles called off the
    men;
And as the dreadnaughts swept to sea, I heard her speaking
    again—

" 'T is hard for the aged and rusty when war sweeps over the
    land!
'T is hard, when others are fighting, for one who has battled
    to stand!
My eight inch guns are useless, but I pray that I still may go,
If not to another 'Manila Bay,' to a splendid grave below!"

ULTIMA THULE.

THE sun, a carmine dagger, wounded the eastern mist;
  The sea, an implacable mirror, glittered with amethyst;
And red dawn raced out fiercely over the restless sweep,
As a keel, a stern war-keel moved out to the burnished deep!

Purple her sails—they were woven out of the glory of dream—
Threaded with light; and their pattern aflame with irradiant
    gleam.
Her oars they shone of silver. Her wake was a boiling gold.
And she surged toward the high loud ocean, where a leaden
    ground-swell rolled.

And what seeks she? In the distance, some white and fabulous
    land?
Curving palms on the hillside? Amber wonderful sand?
Where does she go? To cities splendid with regal worth,
Starred with topaz towers hewn from a lavish earth?

Palaces crumbling and draughty, where only a poppy blows,
Sleepy, nodding, immortal, tinted of flaming rose,—
Where day is a fiery halo, and night is a clear blue wine,
Fragrant, intoxicating, sparkling, crystalline?

Shall the Indian shore allure her, the temples of dusky kings,
Marble fretted with silver, as a white peacock's wings?
Or the slow melodious whisper of a breeze near Pacific isles,
Where the bay is rippled with laughter, the shore is lovely
    with smiles?

Now as she clears the headland; now as she stands to sea;
Speak, O voices prophetic! Where shall her questing be?
For one pale moment she fluttered, sails of shivering light,
Dead on the anxious ocean, dead but gorgeously bright;

Then on the helmsman's face there showed a glance such as
    sea-hawks wear—
The peering eyes, the flinchless gaze, the smile of the hearts
    who dare;

21

And he leaned on the glinting oar that guided the straining
keel,
And the craft leaped madly forward to fly as the gray tern
wheel.

North!—North into the whirlwind!—North to the mocking
gale!
Toward the lash of the driven snowflakes where the scourgèd
sea-dogs quail!
Saw he no ruby towers? Longed not for softer land?
Aye! But a tenser power gripped and directed his hand!

Only a rocky island, drenched in the wildering maze,
Gray through the wreathing blindness, gray in the ghastly
haze!
Iron, frigid, vacant—under the frozen sky;
Where the souls of men become faded, their bodies shrivel and
die!

Not for a princely people!—Mad Cimmerian tribes,
Eyeless, unhuman, horrid, meet him with loathsome gibes;
Not for its argent waters!—Gray and unlovely the waves,
Heaving sullen and formless over the formless graves

Of the men who have striven and lost, of Viking souls who
have dàred,
—Comets snatched by the hungry void whose brilliance no
longer flared!
This is the land he sought: not for the treasure 't would
bring!
The helmsman was of toughening bronze, and wealth is a
chilly thing.

But rather to go where others have not, to conquer where all
have lost,
To battle the frenzied hurricane while Hope is a naked ghost.
Such is the power that drives him into the torturing gale;
This is the rugged goal, this the desired Grail! . . .

So the bright ship moves onward. The tarnished water gleams.
Over the vasty somber space, a liquid sunlight streams.
And all the sea is a molten glow in the imagery of her dreams.

CHALLENGE.

A DIZZY battalion of bronze leaves
   Flickered from the branches that brush the eaves;
While the black wind that hurried after
Reeled with an idiot's empty laughter.
. . . And I who stood in the square below
Swayed with each eddy to and fro
Like a quivering mast in the hurricane,
Till my face was blue with cold and rain.
At last I coughed and rasped my throat
To shatter forth a trumpet note:
"Come, friends of mine, the bellowing gale
Has ripped the clouds as it tatters a sail.
See! In the west a sword of blue
Pierces their chilliness through and through,
And the sun will burst in a yellow haze
To dazzle the hillsides and amaze.
Swift! Harness your mount! We shall ride, ride, ride
Over the saffron countryside.
There are serpents yet to be taught our fear,
And each of us couches a magic spear.
On! youth is ours and hearts of flame
That leap at the sound of a warrior's name;
So let us leave our Camelot
As Gawaine or Sir Launcelot,
Or Geraint for his entrancing Queen.
Over the moor and behind that screen
Of enchanted forest we shall find
Adventure on each flaw of the wind—
A dragon with his blackening breath,
A giant with the arm of death,
A dark knight, glowering by the moat
Of the keep where he's hidden, lonely there,
A damozel with amber hair
That twists like a vine about her throat.
Come! ride on the gale with me, my friend;
We shall find romance at our gallop's end!"

". . . Ah yes, I've mounted my horse!" he cries,
"But the dust o' the road swirls up in my eyes!"

LOST LOVE.

No! I have not seen her again! . . .

After that week of sleet and rain,
You remember, one evening the sun broke through
A rift of the clouds too dripping blue,
And shivered its gold from a hundred spires,
Where the west was smoky and hot with fires!
—That night a something in me shattered,
I know not why! and nothing mattered
Save that I fling from my cage and *go!*
Anywhere, anyhow! So to and fro
I clashed the flags with my stupid pacing,
And sent the hot blood through me racing;
Until a new surge flooded in,
And I turned toward the town with a heart of sin.
And there I walked, insane, unknowing
Whither my crazy course was going;
Brushing the people with tired faces,
Leaving the wind in its giddy races;
With only that sense of a terrible need
To chasten my heart in a burst of speed!

How long I strode thus I cannot tell,
When suddenly (O a silver bell
Rings me back in memory!)
I saw her pass me wonderfully.
An amethyst brooch caught the color of night,
And her dress was satin and faced with white.
I remember this; and remember too
That her delicate look sent a shiver through
My madness. Then she was lost in the crowd!

Gloom drooped upon me as a shroud,
And I turned to my lifeless room in pain! . . .

No! I have not seen her again! . . .

A MEETING.

I. The Man Recalls—

I T was a bleak day, raw and dun!
Grim sun-dogs mocked the hazy sun!

. . . We met in secret on the hill,
Beneath that withered gaunt ash tree
Whose branches like dulled ebony
Whipped overhead against the sky
And, witch-like, creaked most crazily.
We met in secret; none were nigh
To see us toss aloft and spill
The heady wine of youth. (Alas
That these white hours should ever pass
So bitterly, burning on the brain
Only a memory of pain
To rankle!) There we had our fill
Of earthly love, cheek close to cheek . . .
And many hours passed until
The twilight west began to streak
With fire. Then she rose and smiled,
And left me as softly as she came;
And all the sunlight seemed to flame
From the jade-clasped circlet round her hair,
And her glowing cheeks, ah goddess-fair!
As she turned with a nod that spoke me clear:
"Tomorrow night—I shall be here!"

And then—just her presence me beguiled?—
As she flaunted from sight behind the trees,
I felt a tremor; and my knees
Grew weak. A queer revulsion jarred on
My senses. I could never pardon
Myself for silly things I'd done:
O there's no respite to be won
From this! The trees seemed hideous hags,
Disfigured by the touch of sin;
The scraggly thorns they wandered in,

Sharp venomous scorpions, stinging back;
The rocks, gnarled withering dragons black
And scorched.

        O now the world drags, drags!
And still above the hilltops dun,
Grim sun-dogs mock the hazy sun!

II. And She—

1.
And if he does not come again!—
After all I—
        He will, that's plain;
For hear! The bird-note on the bough;
And the clouds have ceased their spatter of rain!
As if man could belie, there is Nature's vow!

2.
Such chance! We might never have met at all!
If I hadn't walked beyond the wall
That, moss-chinked, crosses the pastury hill,
A ruinous thing—just a month ago!
Just a month ago! and the very hour
He happened to choose our road to pass.
I remember a wind shook beads from the grass;
And through ragged clouds, sunlight 'gan to fill
The whitening sky, though day ended slow!

And yet some still grumble there is no Power—
Will see not the sun behind clouds that lower,
Will count not clear days,—only shower on shower
That April bestows on the opening leaves.
And I might have missed him!
              —Well, *one* believes!

REMINISCENCE.

So! Tonight the city is spread like a dream beneath me,
Or a dusky etching traced by the master's hand!
And the wind in the elms has a sleepy song to bequeath me,
But—it blows from the land!

It blows from the land, and I am a-weary of cities,
Weary, too, of the sunset tossed from their spires,
And their rigid outlines—their ardors, their scorns, their
    pities—
And the smoke in sooty gyres.

Their gold is too burnished for me, and each window flaming
Is a vague opal set on a lifeless breast.
—I have seen opals with fire beyond my naming,
Where the surf froths gold in the west!

Nay, but yonder those languid colorous clouds are turning
Idly, like dreaming barques on an enchanted mere,
And all the western towers seem to be burning
Warmly and clear;

And this is beauty you cry. . . . Ah, remember those places
Where the gray beach shows the dimmed end of the land;
And the phosphorescent wash of each wave as it races
Up on the gleaming sand;

And the moonlit sails . . . And still you laugh and deride me,
For drowsing here in the twilight so indolently.
Oh! Though the dark elms were wonderful gods beside me,
Could I forget the sea?

MERLIN.

A LONELY man, his head among the stars
   Walks on the clean sand white beside the sea,—
Merlin, the lonely man of Camelot,
Who left King Arthur and the tournaments
And decorous garlands and the sight of man
Dear to him, yea! the knights and pageantry
To walk beside the waves that curl in foam
And sparkling splendor round him.

                    This because
His vague mysterious power—alchemy
Of mind, by which to purest testable gold
The baser man he strove to elevate
Through curious kabala, muttered words
And formulae, and fiery distillation
Of the elixirs red and white (for this
The allegorists hold to be the sum
And substance of the prime materia,—
Soul-purifier, leaving earth to rest
As 't was)—him lifted flaming far and far
Through unimagined distances of thought
And dream, by pathways metaphysical
To God's own face. And he had seen the face
Of glorious God. And God had looked upon
His eyes.

        So now he walks beside the sea
Alone. And nightly chants he: "I have seen
The Moon, and far beyond her. I have seen
The ringèd planets curve around the Sun,
And the great Sun himself, and far beyond
Strewn stars and stars and filmy nebulae.
Past them across the night, too, have I seen
And known that unapproachable face of God.
And now I walk alone lest man should see
Divinity reflected from mine eyes
Which I am granted only to behold."

Thus Merlin. And the waves around his feet
Break in a fiery phosphorescence, while
The stars above are flaked in fire around,
And the moon floats among them like a barge
Of whitest silver on the unrippled mere.

THE HOUSE OF GOD.

THE organ groans laboriously. A hymn
But half supported by the listlessness
Of many weary voices dwines away
Into the slow dusk shadows. Overhead
The carven cherubs, nodding sleepily,
Smile, half disdainful; while the misty light,
Twisted and shattered by religious panes,
Transmutes the aisles to dusty labyrinths.
Silence—a drowsy murmur—then a man
Pale, bleached, and hazy, steps before the seats,
Compelling sleep in drowsy monotones,
The while he queries vaguely: "Where is God?"

I softly yawn. . . . Where am I? . . . Like a dim
Unhappy dream that dawn turns fugitive,
The arches fade to nothing. Far away
I see the purple gleam of hills and hills
Dipping and curving, graceful, to the sea,
Which like a cerule mirror of the sky
Shows painted clouds and sunset and pure gold.
Now from the west a cool breeze lightly fans,
Whispering songs. Across the silver shield,
Bright ever widening ripples leap away
And all the sea flames points of dancing fire.
Twilight is come. Upon the cheek of dusk
The lovely blushes pale and disappear,
Mantling no more her beauty infinite.
The crumpled clouds assume a bluer shade
Against the lessening orange of the west,
While night flings free her robe of amethyst,
Moon-claspèd o'er the sea. Now the first star
Glints softly as I worship silently. . . .

Where is it? . . . Was I dreaming? . . . With a weight
The intolerable dullness crushes me.
Again, again I see the faded light
And feel the grotesque faces looking down

And laughing mirthlessly. . . . Still the parched voice,
Oppressed by its own impotence drones on
And heavily: "This is God's house!" it says.

REPRISTINATION.

THESE are not God, these spired mounds of stone,
   The grinning gargoyles with their hideous faces,
The clangorous bells that heavily intone
Funereal chiming—sacramental places
Cold as the moon! An altar richly carved
With dead dusk saints—the murmurous drone of prayer—
Atmosphere still, with incense-wreathing scarved—
Dream music—but no Deity is there!

No Deity is there. He rather lingers
In the fresh breeze that cools a lover's cheek,
Or lays at midnight graceful silver fingers
Of moonlight on the ripples of a creek,
Or shouts His chilling loneliness long, long
In the weird cadence of a madman's song!

"ARMA VIRUMQUE—"

COUCHED with Lavinia, close beside the hills
 That are to cradle his empire, grimly waits
Aeneas; and he hears the braggart Fates
Clamoring:—"Lo! our prophecy fulfills
In this scrawn man, this woman of these hills.
From out their loins shall come a race of men,
Brazen in war!" Lavinia flushing thrills,
Snuggling close; then laughs and flushes again;

But he looks widely southward, and he seems
To see great towers piling by the sea,
And a pale queen beneath them. Now he dreams
Another empire. He sighs irritably:
"O I had loved you, proud undestined home!"
But the wind laughs and whips dry leaves toward Rome!

"ANCIENT TO OTHELLO."

IAGO being tortured (runs the tale
  Left incomplete by Shakespeare) nearly dead
In silence, lifted sudden his proud head,
Hair streaming loose, tall cheeks aghast and pale,
Eyes bloodshot. With voice still a sound to quail
His tormentor Cassio, terribly he said:
"Draw close around me, ere my senses fail,
To learn for what my venomy shaft was sped!"

They closed around him. He brushed back his hair
From brow with painful hand. Then slow he moved
His ironic lips, half rose confronting there
The gloating faces,—swift to be reproved!—
Then: "Grammercy for this reprieve—" he cried
"To die in peace!" With this last jest he died.

VIOLINISTS.

H E steps before us all. His fingers seem
   Flames, and most supernaturally white
In the glared brilliance of great chandeliers,
Glassy, ornate, that swing above his head.
A pause . . . the while he seems to sway and sway
Like a bright flower. . . . Suddenly he stands
Erect; and all the air is tide that flows
Rhythmically to the surging of his song.

. . . Poor crazy fiddler, starven, whom the wind
Whimpers around in that gaunt alleyway,
Draggled and cold, how would thy shrivelled heart
Expand for but one glimmering of that flame!

A CHINESE PAINTING.

THE old moon's paling lantern wavers low
  Above the shadow-forests; where the trees,
Forming a ghostly frieze
Of lifted spears against the vacant sky,
Stir restlessly and faintly to the slow
Unquiet shiver of the tremulous breeze.
And O, how ill at ease
The dim place is! For there among the shades
Of leafy vagueness I can see deep eyes
Burning as molten planets with far glow,—
An ancient dragon, twisted, scaly, wise,
Coiled round a treasure, scorning earthly blades.

I draw my sword like some old mandarin,
Fearsomely creeping out against the foe.
And as I rush to strike, my heart within
Chills. He claws snarling. . . . Suddenly the thin
Veil is torn back; and I, half sadly, know
That this is but a dream of what has been—
A cracked old dragon painted long ago.

THE WHITE ROAD.

O N! *Let us take the white road*
   That swerves toward the sea!
The white road that swerves in dust,
Like a serpent, toward the sea!

I.

And one of us saw a peaked roof,
And left the cavalcade
Jaunting along through the hills,—
For the hand of his maid.

Pale ramblers wreathed in the sunlight,
Blown petals drifted the wind,
And the door was deep and dusk,
—He left us riding blind!

II.

And one of us looked on combat,
A king's plume dusty and frayed;
—He left us jogging easily,
And the sunlight hardened his blade.

The trumpets were silver challenges,
The ensigns were crimsoned true,
But we, we rode in laughter
Toward the sea that was bronze and blue.

III.

And one of us knew a mart,
And the droning clamor of trade,
Spread silks for the queen of a Caliph,
Amphorae curiously made.

Gold, gold was strewn on the benches,
Bezant, shekel, doubloon!
And he left us ambling, ambling
Toward the sea that is chill as the moon.

IV.

But some of us rode on
Toward the sea that was carven jade,
Toward the spires and peaks of the haven,
Most splendidly arrayed;

And spires and peaks were phantoms,
The sea was a waste of sand;
Our eyes were mocked with a madness,
Terribly, scornfully grand!

On! let us take the white road
That swerves toward the sea!
The white road that swerves in dust,
Like a serpent, toward the sea!
But O, turn from the white road,
Ere it drop in chill to the sea!

SONG FOR SAINTE-ANNE DES MONTS.

(Grande Rivière.)

OH! Are the Gaspé woodlands still odorous at night?
　　And does the river wheel between most vaguely bright?
Perhaps a salmon flashes from the moonlit pool,
Shimmering below the Northern Light and cool, cool, cool.

In summer; at daybreak, there is a pleasant song
The stream hums softly as it flows along
Through many a foam-white eddy and foam-white fall
Down to the great sea, that knows it all.

In summer, in summer, when the splash of rain
Wakes the tranquil clearness into life again;
And the stream slips round each elbow under dripping leaves,
—O happy is the lilt of the song it weaves!

I have dreamed of it in grandeur—Have you seen the moon
Bulge behind the whipping trees in early June?—
Where the river hurries 'neath them in blue and gold,
And the rich sky is white with stars and very cold.

Or at sunrise, at sunrise, when all the East is wine,
Ruddy for a king's cup, or pavonine
With many, many colors—like gorgeous cloth;
And the little clouds are fringes, or spicy froth.

Have you seen it then? The dawn gusts have crinkled its blue,
And the leaves that overhang it have opals of dew,
And the day is filled with color—like a clear, clear dream,
And the river is a bright sword with faery gleam.

Oh! Are the Gaspé woodlands still odorous at night?
And does the river wheel between most vaguely bright?
And do the birches shift to a sylvan tune?
And the windy pine branches lace the lantern moon?

FOREST CLEARING.

Hard by the stream, where two hills crouched and bent
  Close to each other, whispering evil things,
—Leaves shifting on them like the flutter of wings—
The little road turned rudely down and went
Sharp to the left, a tortuous descent
Past a stripped pine, the windy sentinel
Menacing one bare arm and guarding well
This naked outpost, shivering and rent.

And there the forest broke. A bleak hut stood—
Like a squat toad—upon the gusty plain,
Fringed by the stark gaunt striplings of the wood,
Whereon adventurous the tawny grain
Pushed up. And there the snarled scrub shrank and ran,
As though this were the vanguard of strong man.

THE METROPOLIS.

THE way grew steeper. I uprose
  Past ragged cliff and eager vine
That robed the tenuous incline
With deepest color. Now the close
Of day empurpled each ravine;
While all the hills were giants old
That seemed asleep. Above, the sheen
Of deepening sky impelled me on
To climb where I had never gone
Before. Then sudden, swift and cold,
I felt a wind around me pressed,
And saw the vistas fall away
In tumbled rout.

     And now the crest
Of all was mine . . . and over there,
With gorgeous touch, an idling ray
Made splendid in night's rippling cloak
The dingy mist, the city smoke.
The breeze grew drowsy as a prayer
Scarce formed on lips. The distance flamed
Irradiant glory, deep, unnamed,
A most majestic, silent dream;
And yonder streaked against the sky,
Far off the lights began to gleam.

So all was lovely here; and I
Could pause to view it and to muse:
How new the city was! Its press,
Its crying noise, all undefined,
Had vanished. Now, a pale recluse,
It blazed against the night, enshrined
In visions I could never guess
That it had known. The lights entwined
Their earthlier beauty with the stars—
The Bear, the Hunter, angry Mars—
In wavering points of lucent fire,
Now lower there, now higher, higher;

Until it all grew pale and pale
Before the Moon's invading wave,
Indignant prow and rounding sail
That slashed the clouds, triumphant, brave!

And then I turned around and went
Adown the twisted path I came,
While the proud chilly barque out sent
White halos of transparent flame,
And the great city burned the sky,
A dream of color, gloriously!

WINDY NIGHT.

GREAT crying gusts—and each cloud was a banner,
Harsh bronze, cold silver, smirched with dripping blue,
Fantastic torn, wind-streaming—in the manner
That furious standards blaze above the head
Of battle. Now a hurricane shook through
The tortured branches. All the earth was dead

Around—save I. No!—There the dry leaves crackled!
And—Was it Death himself? I trembled, mad—
A crag-tall figure moved. His laughter cackled,
Crazy with echoes. There! Look there! He strode,
Trampling the pines beneath him as I had
Thin brittle grass. The forest was his road,

Down which he trampled, insolent, rash, swaying
The crushed chill slopes with his affronting feet;
Then paused awhile—the wide-mouthed gale was baying!—
To blow his purpled fingers. Bah! The cold
Was fierce that night! A senseless whirl of sleet
Maddened his pathway. Terrible and old

His weathered face, storm-creased! He stopped, and flinging
His bulk against a mountain, clamored loud
To all the blasts: who answered, hoarse, unringing
While the soiled night raged horrid with their shout;
Then he crashed on, erect, gigantic, proud,
And the swirled vapors hid him in their rout!

Gone? Was he gone? The rent clouds raced insanely;
Foul dusk boiled up, all turbulent with fear
And wildered breath. Yet cold revulsion vainly
Strove at my heart. For suddenly—too soon
For dread—the frayed mists vanished. White and clear
Above the ragged pines was blazed the moon!

THE WIND.

THE wind is full of poetry. At night
    It whispers songs around the drooping eaves.
Sometimes it ripples softly through the leaves,
Making low music, delicate and light,
Drifting the clouds and turning to a bright
And starry dream the sky. It richly weaves
A colored fable no one e'er believes,
Winging its fancy to a lyric height.

I have desired to sing as does the wind,
Murmuring placidly among the trees,
And see its sights. For it has oft reclined
In breathless Eastern cities, where the breeze
Comes as a smile of God from gentle seas,
Refreshing with its touch the feverous mind.

SONG.

I.

I SHOULD like to think of life as the coming of quiet,
—O, a growing awhile,—then rest and ardor together,—
A strolling afar from the tide and its choppy riot,
  In a glory of April weather!

II.

I should like to turn from the surf and its spume that hisses,
Finding life and splendor and love in the sleepy hills—
Where the sun-slopes are crammed with bright bluebells,
    where wonderfully kisses
  The breeze with a calmness that thrills!

III.

But the sea is stronger than all. On a noisy lee shore
My heart must watch the foam pile. Life must be for me
As a salty blast of wind by the stormy seashore,
  As a frenzy of waves from the sea!

SEPTEMBER SONG.

COME with me! The autumnal moon is flooding
  Dead rose petals with silver tonight.
Come from within! This is not the time to be brooding
By the hearth's tremulous light.

The marge of the pond—in June there were lilies drifting—
Is darkened by the gusty breeze;
This is the miraculous time of the season's shifting,
When the leaves turn flame on the trees.

Come! And leave your songs and your dusty fancies
To crumble. The clouds are calling you. Haste along!
What need, O friend, for the glamour of old romances
Now, when the night is a song?

ON A GLOOMY DAY.

AND April's opening buds were slashed with rain;
And April's hopeful flowers were harried back;
And the bursting dogwood dared not show,—
Only the poplars with their woe,
And the willows with their pain!

And April's glorious singers stifled their breath;
And April's shower of odes were uncomposed;
And the lyric of streamlets could not be,—
Only the ocean's threnody,
And the loud waves' promise of death!

PRELUDE.

Come with the quivers of light
  To waken the soul of day!
Come, come away!
Dawn is softly stirring under the flaming hills,
Night is wearily nodding over the paling hills,
And the stars have fled away.
Whisper a song of morning
To startle the fleeing night!
For the wan blue clouds are blowing
And the sky is bright.
Sing, sing, sing! Sing with the voice of the years:
The red sun creeps o'er the hilltop to scatter your hopeless
    fears!

PASTORAL.

Listen! Listen!
There from that blossomy spray a-glisten
With crowded yellow forsythia flowers,
A spurt of singing throbs out, overpowers
The sloth of my heart!
From that thicket of brambles dart
A flutter of sparrows, dipping by!
And up in the clearness of clear blue sky
Three hoarse old crows flap, high!

SWIMMING AT NIGHT.

JUST a race in the dusk around the hill,
  Past two tall pines that fringe the moon,
A crackle of stones—then a tang of still
Bay-pungent air. And the cool beach glows,
White as the stars, beneath my feet,
And reflects in light on the long lagoon.

I walk to the rim of the burnished sheet,
—The water's touch is a goddess' hand—
Then the splashy wavelets leap in rows
As I swim away from the darkening land!

WINTER SEA.

Who hath not heard the sea on windy nights
    Mournfully sob a sullen threnody
Around the coast? Who hath not heard it moan?
Its ceaseless waves that sweep before the gale
Hammer the cliffs in sorrow pitiless
While dusk November holds the iron shore
In grasp tyrannic? Yond the sea gulls shriek
And in their strident cries I seem to hear
Barbaric voices wailing through the gloom,
Mourning the ages: old Icelandic ghosts
That weep wild sagas in the thralling mist
Of Leif the Lucky's war keels long ago.

SONNET.

THE lucent walls of Rome, bards oft have praised,
　　Thronging bronze-towered on the sacred hills;
And in some hearts surpassing rapture thrills
At Nineveh's old wonder. Men have raised
Vast rhythmic songs to Athens' temple, blazed
Sun-golden, as a coronal, above
Her poetry and splendor . . . By a love
Of these sure beauties, man shall be appraised.

But O, the silver foam about the prows
Of Tyrian ships that float before the breeze
Past Sicily and onward, over seas
Turquoise and lovely, which their oars arouse
To opalescent glitter, as they drowse
At sunset through the gates of Hercules.

TO A PLATONIST.

I KNOW you love to wander far from things,
  By soul-paths out beyond the flaming orbs
Of heaven. Yes, I know pure thought absorbs
Your splendor. And you laugh, come face to face
With God, at earth—exultantly, and race,
Wheeling on fiery wings.

But oh, oh! walk with me at eventide
Down the dimmed street; look wonderfully with me
Upon the people's faces. You will see
Man grown resplendent, glorious, divine,
Man's work that sheds the sunlight like soft wine,
And holy God beside!

PEACE: A MEMORY.

IT seems so long; 't was but three years ago—
   Three fleeting years of sunshine and of rain—
When it had not begun; nor all the pain
And hate had come. The world that now we know
Was yet unborn. The mornings come and go,
The air today is just as soft as then—
That spring three years ago. But ne'er again
Will be so bright the summer's hallowed glow.

And yet, perhaps, when all the strife is o'er,
Such of us then as still survive may drift
Into those idle ways we knew before
The bloody years. If this be so some shift
Of unseen wind, I pray, shall stir and lift
The mist and give us memory of war!

   June, 1917.

PEACE.

(June 28, 1919.)

THERE was a drawn, mad silence in the room
    Where grouped forms moved as shadows quietly—
Pale as the fog that slides in from the sea
At dawn. The air was sodden—of a tomb—
And dull. A sable judge invoking doom
Upon the culprit (So he seemed that sate
On the proud dais of the victorious state)
Murmured, and two ghosts signed, and fled in gloom. . . .

And there were other things—unseen. Vague rows
Of naked graves that stretched across the lands,
White torn homes, and dream-shattered hopeless hands,
Starting blind eyes that groped and could not see,
And—reaching ghastly arms to part the foes—
A mute bare cross upon Gethsemane.

AFTER COMBAT.

Hark! Yonder elm-tree seems to pulse with singing
   That fire has hardly spared. Hark! Do I hear
The mavis-note in that seared bracken ringing,
No trace of fear?

The rank grass strives to hide the hideous scourings
Of blundering man. The e'er-immortal earth
Re-flowers to life—despite unlovely lowerings—
In clearer birth.

Was it a dream—so little seems regretted,
While more, more gorgeousness comes on us soon—
That I saw spearmen, last night! silhouetted
Against the moon?

THE WHITE GOD.

THE WHITE GOD.

(Quetzalco-atl.)

THE great prince Montezuma, swerving back
 From a victorious raid on Yucatan,
—(In this his serpent standards had advanced
To Nicaragua lake)—was troubled. He
Had heard rude murmurs fanning from the coast,
And whispers of rebellion bruited far,
And word of mad forewarnings wafted far,
On every gust that blew from Mexico.

So as he passed through Xoloc, hastening
To Tenochtitlan of the many roofs,
His glistening city, all his mind was stirred
With turbulent brooding; and he looked not out
Upon his dusky subjects, gathering
With flowers and luting to adorn his path
Of triumph to the capitol. Within
His gold-encrusted palanquin he sat,
Despondent, irritable, while his ears
Rang with this gloomy clamor: all has gone!
And as the crowds cheered closer, he recoiled
And sank against the cushions, crass and dull
And heavy, and his vision seemed to blur
Into a streak of unreality
That confused all things vaguely, as in dream.
Then first the sunlit towers became a haze,
Shimmering and dizzy; then the hopeless throng,
A sea that hammered one black cliff,—insane,
Surging against its feet in spume, and broken,
Hurrying back in nebulous cascades
On which the sunlight flashed and turned to red.
Until at last new waves of huger bulk
Rose from the East and battered hard and long,
And battered hard and troubled loud and boiled,
Fuming around the cliff which shivered, rent,
And tottered, and then fell. And all the rocks
Fell with it; and the sloping mountainside.

Then Montezuma woke and saw he moved
Adown the flinty causeway to the isles
Of his great templed city. And the crowds
Yet seethed around him, gliding ever near,
Hovering close in garlanded canoes
To fling bright roses at his feet, and cry
"Live emperor! Live conqueror!" So he,
Exalted by their rapture, proud arose
And shook his green plumes lightly overhead
This sweep of luxuriant color, and he spoke:
"My children, thunderous deeds shall come of you!"
Then he passed on to enter gloriously,
And laughed and babbled with his retinue,
And laughed and jested more a man than king,
Until one cry disturbed them all, bayed out:
"The White God shall return!"

       The king rebuked
That ominous echo, in the council hall,
Thereafter. And proclaimed it death to him—
If any found—who shouted. Yet the wail,
Mocking and mocking, troubled still and leered,
Reverberant. That night a comet flared
Over Quetzalco-atl's shrine. The hills
Shook dully: while a flaming blazed the East—
Whither he sailed in old time. And that cry:
"The White God shall return!"

       And Montezuma
Was cowed by that incessant hovering wail
Of the end of things; and knew not what to do.
Until Cacama came to him—the same
Whom he had lifted to the eagle throne
Of white Tezcuco—and he said: "My lord,
These prophecies have raised great stir against you,
And against me as friend to you. For all
Whom fear has ever silenced, now—damned curs!—
Scheme to make head against you. Cempoalla,
Cholula, Puebla—these will cast aside

Their watery bond and weld by insurrection
Sure faith with the Tlascalans. And perchance
My brother will move southward to assault
Tezcuco, hoping in the ruin of all
To gain himself a princedom. O these times!
When all we cherish shivers on the brink
Of an unbottomed cavern! Aye, my lord!
Coyotes yelp around. I hear, I hear
Their coward challenge slink among the hills,
And see their green eyes glowing in the dusk,
And feel their breathing. Snatch a brand, my lord,
Sputtering from the fire and scare them back,
Ere they gorge upon our carrion!"

                        And the king:
"Cacama, I did well to give you rule.
Now teach me, from your inspiration, how
May this loud storm be driven from the sea?"
And Prince Cacama: "I but spoke in haste,
Admonishing you to fright them, petulantly.
Then would they herd for safety. O my king,
Let me recount a dream. It seems therein
I read a parable. Last night it was—
And still is clear as glory—yes, last night
I saw a cypress clinging to the verge
Of a tall precipice that overawed
The Chalcan lake. And as I looked, a gale,
A wet tornado gathering from the Gulf
Stormed menacing upon the chiselled crests
Of other hills, and muttered threateningly.
Then thunder clattered hoarsely like the wheels
Of ponderous chariots. Lightning ripped and tore
The blue banked clouds. But still the cypress stood—
Its leaves a-quiver—only these—no more.
At last the wind coursed outward from the vale,
Tear-glistening. The thunder droned away.
The white swords flashed more vaguely. And again
The earth knew peace. It was more dear, thrice dear
For all the turmoil. After, I awoke;

And heard the dread cry clamor through your halls:
'The White God shall return. Quetzalco-atl
Tramps in the fateful East!' And I arose
And came to you. Dire prince, these times of ours
Are grievous. And you ask me—how shall you
Withstand their onset? Sire, yon tree is there,
Sky-tracing, lovely-shadowed. You must stand
Unmoved, as it stood, with its leaves a-quiver;
And this great storm will clatter into distance;
The earth know peace again. We do not deal
With men, with men alone—"

                  Again the king
Broke in to query: "This same tree of yours,
How shall it guide me? Do you mean I stand
Aloof, unmindful that the broils of men
Topple my empire? Do I read you well?
Or how? Or what?" Cacama swift replied:
"Its leaves a-quiver, wise my lord, I said.
On this may hang your acts." And turned away,
And left King Montezuma on his throne,
Perplexed and pondering,—and he sat that way,
Perplexed and pondering, till the sun dropped down,
And a young moon climbed brightly overhead.

    Not overlong thereafter he convoked
A ponderous council—Prince Cacama first,
And Cuitlahua, his own warlike brother,
And Nezahual-pilli, a priest of the gods.

    And all the while, wave-slashing, on there drove
Ten caravels across the Cuban seas
Toward Cozumel.

             For Alvarado—he
Later called Tonatiuh by the men
Of Aztlan, for his god-surpassing frame
And lustrous hair—had hurried back before
Grijalva, bearing rumors of a land
Of gold, perchance great fabled El Dorado.

64

And later when Grijalva came he spoke
Of the great Mayan strongholds, and the gold
Curiously worked, and showed them pendant stones
Of intricate setting. And he said: "My lord,"
—This to Velasquez, Cuba's governor,
Iron of brow, who swayed the vice-regal rod
As though it were a sceptre: leering man—
"My lord, beyond this land they pointed north
And westward, while they cowered shiveringly,
And paled—if these men ever pale—and howled:
'Colhua! O Colhua!'—like the wind
Restively chafing all the topmost trees,
Cypress or cedar; after that no more
Would speak—as though it were a sacrilege
To speak at all. And then we onward moved
Through the snarled primal forest, while the scrub
Grew barbed and menacing. Great tortuous groves
Of ceiba, labyrinthine, tangled us.
And there were flowers unknown and glorious.
And then we splashed through marshes simmering,
And crossed black serpent streams that interwound
Among the slimy roots malarial;
Near other forest cities. Ever all
'Colhua! O Colhua!' cried, and north
And westward pointed—till at length we came
To a last river deeper than the rest,
Too deep to ford, sea-moving, languorous.
Here all the banks were oozy, overhung
With dripping vines, entangled, poisonous.
And 'cross it thick impregnable undergrowth
Twisted and thorny barred our strong advance.
All, all was evil! And behind the brush—
More evil yet—I saw the glint of spears,
The shift of plumes that rippled in the gusts,
The brassy ensigns. And my guides slunk back
Into the shadows close around the camp,
And quivered terror-palsied, and breathed out:
'Colhua! O Colhua!'—and (methought)
Fearfully: 'Montezuma!'—hoarse with dread;

Then pointed north and westward to the host
That held the farther shore, and huddled in
Around us. So the night was passed in fear!

"And when the dawn, bespangled, tremulous,
Shone on the trailing branches, tremulous,
To wake the captains, lo! the host was gone,
And all the gaudy jungle hushed. A burst
Of windy exultation shattered through
Our drawn blanched ranks, while our swords flashed and
     blazoned
Pale lightnings in the sunlight, and outrang
In surgent thunder, iron, clamorous.
And now I was uncertain where to turn.
Three hundred men I landed with. But some
Were dead beside the shore, and some were dying,
And others feverous. And yet that dream—
The fitful wind had blown me—and the gold,
And the far whispers of a jewelled city
Beyond—perchance great fabled El Dorado!
Scarce knew I where to turn? By faith! I knew
That night! For Captain Alva, foraging
In the jungle, chanced upon a feathery band
Of Mexicans, accoutred all for war.
He fell upon them sharply, imprisoning
Their leader, a plumed cacique, him haling in
To me. We could not speak his barbarous tongue;
But we had with us one—rescued before
By Alvarado—who had lain among
The Mayans, a prisoner for twenty years.
He was a Spaniard; and he yet recalled
Brokenly the speech, Castilian, of his birth.
Through him we talked. The chief was loath to tell
Of his dark business and the empery
Of that proud king he served. But—having learned
From the poor Spaniard torturing would avail
Little against his slavish loyalty—
We tried persuasion, told him of our king
Past the engirdling sea, and urged that he

Would tell us of his lord, that we might go
Spain-wards to bear the brother monarch tiding
Of this rich Western king.

                   "The Mexican
Grew flame-eyed, pointing astounded at the sea,
And cried: 'Quetzalco-atl! Dost thou come
After these years?' And pressed in adoration,
Telling us all. Of Montezuma, lord
Of a sea-stretching empire, and the cities
Servile to him, and princes: young Cacama,
Scarce less to him, who served him faithfully.
And how one city, ringed by snowy hills
Down which the blue streams filtered wanderingly,
A coronal of marble, Tenochtitlan,
Was proud beyond all cities, and absorbed
The whole realm's glory; silver from the veins
Of dusky caverns, opals, amethysts,
Gold from the spattering streams, and luxury.
How from a western ocean was borne up
Spice from the invisible isles behind the mist;
Tamarinds from the tropics, from the Gulf
Fishes all-golden for the Emperor's fare.
And how Tlascala stood alone against
The conquests of this king, fierce proud republic
Girdled by him, unbowed, within her mountain
Like a dun rattlesnake hissing, coiled to strike,
And venomous. For Montezuma's armies
Were many-numbered as the sanguine flowers
That make his vale a troublous mere of blood—
Armored and gaudy, showering with arrows
And spears the whole broad country and the gods
Of who opposed them, till Tlascala sole
Defied. And that the gods of Aztlan were
Blood-terrible and ravenous, who all clamored
Intolerably for death and sacrifice
And rutilant altars, charred with misery:
Save one—Quetzalco-atl—he had passed
Across our sea, but one day would return,

White visaged; and how we must be the sons
Of this god. And perchance our king was he.
And then he said the nearest vassal city,
The river washed, Tobasco, heard report
Of warriors moving and our sun-bright trappings
And thundery missiles. She was fitting out
Imperial expedition—myriad strong—
To oppose our progress, to subdue and drag
Our captains to the altars to allay
The terrible portents which the Lord of War
In wrath had hurled on Aztlan, while he shook
The heart of Montezuma with his ire.
(For ghastly stars had blazed across the night,
Firing the streaky heavens, and those mounds
Wherein the dead were buried, gaped anew,
Hell-yawning, and discharged the fleshless ghosts
On palsied Tenochtitlan, bellowing
With fear and frenzy as the inhabitants read
God's supernatural scrawl upon the clouds,
Presaging ruin!) And they deemed, he said,
The fiery Tobascans, that suddenly
To seize and slay us all in sacrifice
Might regain favor with the god. They lay
Nearly a sea league onward and were drawn
Into array of combat. Did we move
Forward—on this their hope was set—destruction
Would blaze upon us from an ambuscade.

"How might our hundreds plunge against that throng,
My lord Velasquez? What could I do else
Than this I did? For summoning a council
Of Alva, Alvarado and the rest,
I made them known of all, acquainting them
With this I tell you. We deliberated
Gravely—without decision. Till there came
Returning scouts, who told us on a rise,
Wooded, beyond the river, there were thrown
Multitudes ranged in combatant align;
And that they skirmished with an outpost, where

One Spaniard, being wounded, sickened, died
Horribly with fierce torture on his face
Blue-black with poison. After this no doubt
Remained in us. We hastened to withdraw,
Embarqued anew, and set our prows toward Cuba."

"O for a heart of flame!" Velasquez cried.
And then no more, but held him silently
From vehement outburst, chewing at his fingers
Savagely. Till at length the powder flared
With sudden explosion. And the governor's soul
Raged—most insanely. And he stood erect
While tremulous lightning flickered from his eyes,
And a gale shuddered the tempestuous hills
Less harshly than his voice. "Grijalva, I
Entrusted much to you. And you slink back,
Dishonored and a coward! O fool, fool!
With victory half-compassed to retreat—
Stupidly. Coward! I have wasted much
On friends. Perchance in this a venturous foe
Will serve me better. Take the faint-heart off,
Soldiers, to prison. Summon me Cortez,
That fortunate ruffian valorous at best!"

And as they passed they almost hear him murmur
"Gold!"—like a dream, and start within himself
Too nervously. And twitch his yellow thumbs,
And again murmur "Gold!"

                              That night Cortez
Came stealthily to him; and he addressed
The rebel: "Cortez, you have been my foe
Irreconcilable through many years,—
Seditious, slanderous,—I will speak you frank—
Treasonable to Spain, disloyal to
Her king; but above all things valorous!
A thunder-brand in Cuba, devastating;
Hateful as the dun wolf that wantonly

Raids the weak foothill outposts, pitiless;
But—beyond all men!—ever valorous!
Touching rebellion, I forgive you that.
Little I need forgive, since you have been
Untrammelled by my enmity; and touching
Your Catalina—there I could not yield,
For honor—you have married her, so I
Am free to act: I give forgiveness too.
For this return: that you equip a fleet,
—I sharing in the maintenance,—and profit—
To carry war against the western empire
Of Aztlan that Grijalva has found out!"
And Cortez answering: "Forgiveness keep
For those who crave forgiveness. Yet you speak
Fairly—for you, Velasquez. So I yield
To you in courtesy. This night I ride
To my plantations, mustering my men
For conquest. Swift returning I shall come
With warriors and gold to bear you out
In this tremendous enterprise of iron!"
Then strode away. And in the quivering light
Velasquez sat—as in a sun-spilled cave,
Mountainous with gold, and all the dusk swirled round
His senses, spattered golden where the stars
Were gold upon the deepness of the night.

Then two days after, Cortez hurried back
With warriors and gold—and the small haven
St. Iago, cutting back among the hills,
Grew glistening with life. Its hollowed cup
Filled to the brim with life—adventurers,
Gold questers from the island San Domingo,
Slavers and soldiers, ruffians of fortune,
Brigands—and pompous priests; for this high mission
Was a crusade, and many a sorry native,
Benighted in idolatry and evil
And desperate worship, would be won to light
And to the Cross. The expedition gained
In prestige and glory. And the caravels,

70

Cloud-stately, moored beneath the enclosing hills,
Chafed at their cables, tugging to be free.

But all the while Cortez more haughty seemed,
As might become a princeling. And Velasquez
Grew restless and uneasy. So the foes
Of the new captain, sensing cautiously
A chance for treachery, whispered in the night
Persuasive words; said Cortez would be king
In Mexico. Or if not king, would rob
Velasquez of his primacy. Already—
They could confide—the leader imperious grew,
And insolent, and despising of the power
Of Cuba's governor. These whispers crept
Envenomed to Velasquez' credulous ear;
Then in a flaw of anger he cried out
Against the adventurer. And these enemies,
Stealthy, of Cortez played upon the fury,
And pressed him to remove the proud command,
Giving the fleet to them.

                           But fortunately
Young Lares and Duero, councilors
Of state, discovered this new mad decision.
They hurried to Cortez, and bade him fly.
And he, the brave, despised not listening;
Nor obdurate was, but thought of Mexico.
So secretly, ere dawn, he hoisted sail
Darkly above the phosphorescent bay.
And at the sunrise bellowed a farewell
To Velasquez and turned seaward suddenly.

And so it came, wave-slashing, that there drove
Ten caravels across the Cuban sea
Toward Cozumel.

                    And at this time the king
Convoked his council—Prince Cacama first,
And Cuitlahua, his own warlike brother,
And Nezahual-pilli, a priest of the gods.

71

And when they came, he breathed them the ill-ease
That festered in his soul—the hideous dream,
Bat-winged, that flittered duskly through the night
Down all the timorous archways of his mind;
And, more than all, that quaver of despair:
"The White God shall return!"—and cried to them
Distractedly: "I know not what to do.
Gladly I would forget, most gladly would
I clatter away in a burst of ridicule
These nightmares. But my hour for mirth has passed.
Ironically the favor of our gods—
Leaving a blasted trail too like the passage
Of an outrageous army—sweeps along
To lure another victim with its hope,
And then to blot him most destructively,
That promise of hope consumed. I'm like a hawk
Half wounded by a shaft's inaccuracy,
Who flutters on awhile, at last droops down,
Wracked by more torment than the torturing arrow's—
His little hurt become the death of all!
O misery, misery! Cacama, you have been
A comforter and prop to my misgivings
Ere now. Read you my heart? What shall I do?"

And young Cacama: "Lord, you haste to move
With ill control, perchance to your undoing,
In what is but an apprehended dream!
Sorrow enough in life. Make not you dreams
Uncomfortable pain, that are the solace
Alike of challenging youth and testy age.
Make not of dreams—! Pour not so glorious strength
In maddening the disconsolate heart of yours
Too sorely. You will drive it fierce to bay;
And then the whole will crumble! I who bore
First whisperings of turmoil, beg you wait!
Wait, and then wait, my lord!" But Montezuma
Smiled at his prayer, and thus indulgently:
"Ha! Youth can live on this! and breathe, and thrive;
Drink, draw repose, and surer manlier strength.

72

You have said well—not wisely. Look! Awhile,
(And you have said!) first whispering of upheaval
You carried me. I troubled, and you came.
And now you tell me peace. No! I must hold
First words the more inspired. Cuitlahua,
What say you to my dreams?"

His brother replied:
"I only hold a sword in my right hand.
I only wear a buckler on my arm.
If there be need of else,—why, turn from me!
Seek you some shrewd adviser. Yet, my lord,
Why race Time toward the future to confront
The impending pain of years? You hold a sword,
Wind-sharp to strike! And if a man oppose,
Then let him feel its blade,—and if a god,
Fear not to try him too. Stand easily,
Until the hour shall challenge. Then, my king,
Strike hard, strike swift, and I will strike for you!"

Him Montezuma: "Counsel much the same
Flares from your laudable fire. But, O my brother,
This heart misgives me. Nezahual-pilli,
Read you the terrible auguries of heaven
And bear right witness of the future. I
Misdoubt my hopes. Say what the gods have scrawled
In skyey script, imblazoned 'mong the stars!"

(And Cuitlahua unto Prince Cacama,
Aside: "In verity, now shall we hear
A welter of disaster; for these priests,
If they be versed—as this knave surely is—
In priestly ways, have learned to make of fear
Their heritage of weal." And Prince Cacama,
Likewise aside: "So is it, as you say.")

And Nezahual-pilli the while was still,
Eyes rolled to heaven, with dumb lips and blank

Expressionless ghastly visage, in a trance—
Thence subject to the subtlest influence
Of inspired word. At length he dashed aside
His stupor—though in a coma strangely still—
And spurned his tragic silence and cried out
With frenzy—god-impassioned into song:

"Not in a wattled and dreamy barque,
—So have the gods cried—(Hark! O hark!)
Drifting the quiet indolent seas;
Not on the pale, pale Western breeze
Wafted,—with prayers and the favor of man,—
Quetzalco-atl's voyage began
Sunward across the seas!

"There! Do you hear them? The hissing of snakes!
Silence! O silence! The stillness breaks
As man, the fool, drives forth in rage
His saviour god. Lo! the heritage
Shall be reeling woe when the god returns;
For his wrath is a sputtering brand that burns,
The god man drove forth in rage!

"Bearing a gift of reason he came
Over the hills with an aureole of flame,
And wheat in his hand, and twisted gold,
And a touch of fire to charm the cold
From man.—Scourged forth his flight begins
In a poisonous craft of serpent-skins,
He that brought wheat and gold!

"O fools! Stark fools! with your lashes hot
Flaying and driving you knew not what!
With a sword in your hands and chill blue steel
In your senseless hearts! Will you never feel
The presence of God? Too late! He comes,
Murderous to the throb of drums,
The god you have shown with steel!"

74

Swift, like a sob outwept, his clamorous song
Subsided, and a quietude suddenly
Surged in for few white moments; till the priest
Aroused from his dazed silence, thundering:
"Yes! By the gods! 'T is so! Quetzalco-atl
Departs in rage. In rage he shall return
Shortly. And give this empire to the sword
Of his pale children. On the eastern sea
Their ships are pressing boldly—even now!
The end has come. Your empire falls in dust,
And rust shall rivel all those palaces
Of yours, O king!" Then with a convulsive moan,
He sank upon the floor, and wept, and wept.

After that wail of anguish, Montezuma
Blanched for a moment as the priest had done,
Blanched, looking vacantly about the room
Wherein the council sat. But suddenly
His color blazed back. Then, wheeling to his brother,
He said: "And I shall need your sword some day!"
Then faltered (while he looked upon the priest)
Then laughed, and to Cacama laughingly:
"Poor superstitious! These be prophecies?
I like your counsel better." And no more.

  * * * * *

Off Yucatan that night there fluttered in
A wildered ship, storm-draggled, wearily;
And after her nine others. And they dropped
Most wearily their anchors, and drew in
Like sleeping swans, close to the Mexican shore.